A Family of Poets

A Family of Poets

The Poetry of

Margaret Mary Jones Strope

and Her Children

Mahlon Brewster Strope, Jr.

Marvin Bernard Strope

Sandy Strope Hill

Joanne Lee Strope Pelton

Lynne Strope Jonas

Ivan Floyd Strope

iUniverse, Inc.
New York Lincoln Shanghai

A Family of Poets
The Poetry of Margaret Mary Jones Strope and Her Children

iUniverse books may be ordered through booksellers or by contacting:

iUniverse
2021 Pine Lake Road, Suite 100
Lincoln, NE 68512
www.iuniverse.com
1-800-Authors (1-800-288-4677)

Back photo, clockwise from top: Mahlon Brewster Strope Jr., Marvin Bernard Strope, Joanne Lee Strope Pelton, Lynne Strope Jonas, Sandy Strope Hill, Ivan Floyd Strope

ISBN: 978-0-595-47238-3 (pbk)
ISBN: 978-0-595-91520-0 (ebk)

Printed in the United States of America

In loving memory of our mother

Margaret Mary Jones Strope

1912–1960

Margaret Mary Jones Strope
~ 1946

Contents

Introduction

Margaret Mary Jones Strope spent much of her too-brief life raising six children, during the difficult years of the Great Depression and World War II, and still found time to write poetry. She bequeathed to her offspring her love of the written word and a sense of the power of poetry to express the inner, sometimes unsuspected, thoughts and emotions of the writer. She was born in 1912 in Syracuse, N.Y., married Mahlon Brewster Strope Sr. in 1930, lived most of her life in Towanda, Pa., and died in 1960, of complications from asthma. Although this volume contains some of her work, sadly, most of her poetic writing has been lost. This book is a tribute to her and an acknowledgement of her legacy: A family of poets.

Mahlon Brewster Strope Jr. is a retired chemist who has recently moved to North Carolina with his wife, Karen. Brewster has written approximately 400 poems and numerous short stories.

Dr. Marvin Bernard Strope is retired from the College of Southern Idaho as Dean of Academics. He and his wife, Ingrid, split their time between their Florida home and their cabin in Idaho on the Salmon River.

Sandy Strope Hill is semi-retired as an editor of the Charlotte Observer. Sandy and her husband, Dennis Carrigan, are both writers.

Joanne Lee Strope Pelton is a retired Registered Nurse living in Virginia with her husband, Raymond.

Lynne Strope Jonas lives in North Carolina, with her husband, Richard, and raises and trains horses.

Ivan Floyd Strope lives in North Carolina with his wife, Patricia, and is an independent sales representative providing environmental protection systems.

Love & Friendship

God's Roommate

My soul delights to hear her
sing praises to the King,
in tones that angels envy,
and would that they could sing.

Her hurting for the helpless
proclaims the One within,
reveals her soul as selfless,
surrendered unto Him.

He knew her inner beauty
and so set her apart.
In sovereign love He made her
His roommate in my heart.

Ivan Floyd Strope

The Box

A brass box lives on my dresser
oval as an eye 3 inches long.
Stamped on the bottom, "Made in Taiwan"
Lamplight gleams warm on 30 years of touching,
warm as the August afternoon you gave it to me,
a talisman for college,
crammed full of kisses, 200 of them,
ready to be taken out and applied as needed
for lonely nights, exam days, flu.
No new kisses are possible now.
When I open the box,
sometimes a stray kiss floats out
and leaves a warm spot on my cheek,
potent as ever.

Sandy Strope Hill

High Places

(Written for my twin brother, "the adventurer.")

I have trod the high places
Where heaven brushes earth,
It seems that I have sought them
From the moment of my birth.

Volcanoes in Hawaii
Kilimanjaro's peak
The Valley of the Moon
Places with wild mystique.

I've climbed the Sawtooth Mountains
Made the rocks my berth
I've seen the source of Angel Falls
And walked the roof of earth

And when I pass the gates of pearl
I shall not stop close by,
Just long enough to ask Saint Pete,
"Where do the mountains lie?"

Mahlon Brewster Strope Jr

Dying Young

The tragedy you see
is not that you died,
but that you were so young.
And so was I.
Talking to a tombstone
is so unsatisfactory.

Sandy Strope Hill

Silence Spoken Here

I sit awash in the gleam of my screen,
my fingers caressing these plastic keys,
composing, supposing you understand
the depth of my love your eyes never see.

While you are lost in pages of yore
and deeds not possible for mere mortals,
written by one who would steal your amour
and besiege your heart's unguarded portals.

What do we seek with our own distractions?
Why don't we say the words said in the past?
What, pray tell, has become of our passion?
When will we sever this cycle at last?

Just one more line and I will be through, dear.
Just one more page to the end of the book.
Just a bit longer and I'll draw you near.
Why don't you just stay right there in your nook?

Finally, I found the time to hold you.
At last, I said what you wanted to hear.
Too bad, too late, too little to matter.
I found the time but you're no longer here.

Ivan Floyd Strope

Long Distance Love

My love and I talk on the phone
And then hang up and are alone.
'Tis bittersweet this love we've sown.
I'd not begun if I had known.

Mahlon Brewster Strope, Jr.

For Sandy and Lynne

I stand and watch the hills on fire,
with colors scarlet, flame and gold.
I laugh and push the years aside
and like the hills, grow gay and bold.

I watch for you, so near and dear,
so long and far away.
For you and me the glory sings
in woods where we did play.

I cannot say what changes are,
what different paths we go.
But come each fall in golden woods
and three are there I know.

Joanne Lee Strope Pelton

Honey Bee

I don't know where you are today,
I won't know on tomorrow.
Our love is gone and blown away,
And gone both joy and sorrow.

But still somehow you're in my heart;
One bee in fields of clover.
And now and then you buzz my thoughts;
A memory not over.

Mahlon Brewster Strope Jr.

Two Years After
(5/08/2004)

This razor's edge is blunted now.
I scarce can feel the pain,
'til something comes with a leather strap
and hones the blade again.

Joanne Lee Strope Pelton

Without

Without him, the taste has gone flat
of wearing perfume
and
reading in bed
and walking in woods

Without him, the glow has gone out
of baking a pie
and
wishing on stars
and
me.

Joanne Lee Strope Pelton

Almost a Friend

He was small of stature
with childlike hands
and soft eyes
set in an elfish face.

Not a man's man,
humble of spirit,
so very gentle.

I never heard him
speak a harsh word,
for I do not believe
such a word would find
a home in his heart.

Just a distant relation
and now he's gone
without warning.

I think I will miss him a bit.

I wish I would miss him more.

Ivan Floyd Strope

Visiting After A Loss

We perch on the couch
admiring your new blue slipcovers.
I want to say,
"I'm sorry about Bob."
But you chatter on
behind a perfect smile,
"Now the corners, they're rounded, see
and they were the hardest things to do."
"They're beautiful," I say. *"Blue*
was Bob's favorite color."
And you look at me fawn-startled
and talk about the weather.

Sandy Strope Hill

Separation

I think my heart is breaking—is yours?
It's getting harder
It's getting colder
It's beating with such pain
I think my heart is breaking—is yours?

Joanne Lee Strope Pelton

Comfort

Do not despair, my own sweet heart,
For help is on the way.
My long, strong arms will comfort you,
My love will save the day.

Joanne Lee Strope Pelton

Trio for Leo

My friend, Leo, went home to be with the Lord. Unfortunately, his flesh lingered long after his spirit departed. These were written for him and his faithful wife, Lou. He was a good friend. I miss him.

Home Before Dark (August 17, 2004)

He's almost gone.
The shell remains.
A hollow host
completely drained
of everything
but his name.
The quick wit,
the fellowship
have been replaced
by vacant eyes
that know not me
and helpless hands
that can not move
to play the games
that he so loved.
Oh cruel fate
befall not me
and gentle to
my loved ones be.
Let me be,
please God,
let me be
home before dark.

Ivan Floyd Strope

Almost Home (September 16, 2004)

His heart is failing.
That valiant center
of his being
may not see the dawn.
She's by his side,
where she has been
these many months
with loving hands
never once forsaking.
Yet soon he'll rest
and with a sigh
release them both
to live again.
Not long now.
Not soon enough.

Ivan Floyd Strope

Home at Last (10:40 A.M. Friday, September 17, 2004)

He's not within
this empty shell.
Remember him
as whole and well.
Confusion gone,
all things clear
body strong,
the end of fear.
He waits for us
with friendly smile.
He waits within
eternal now.
You are released,
who so loved him,
to celebrate
his final freedom.
Knowing that,
at journey's end,
the King awaits
our hearts to mend.

Ivan Floyd Strope

Faith & Inspirational

Catechism

(Published March 16, 1945 in Towanda Daily Review)

I thought I knew a lot about
The wonders of the world.
I formed my own philosophies
And walked with them unfurled.
The endless whys and wheres of life
Which man has ever sought,
Enough of these I thought I knew,
But now I know—I only thought.

For how can I pretend to say
My knowledge fits my task
When I falter o'er the questions
A four-year-old can ask:
"Mother, where is Heaven?"
"How high is the sky?"
"What makes the lightning bugs make light?"
"Who made the world and why?"

He asks in all sincerity
This clear-eyed youngster bright,
His trusting face upraised to mine,
For Mother's always right.
I cannot smile or shrug and say,
I've figured thus and so.
Not with my child's clear gaze on mine.
I've really got to know.

Then God in Heaven I realize
How dumb I really am.
I breathe a silent prayer for help
And answer as best I can.
But if while searching for the truth
I lose my smug tranquility,
I have to thank my little son
For teaching me—humility.

Margaret Mary Jones Strope

The Rainbow
(Published May 23, 1946 in the Towanda Daily Review)

He has set his bow in the sky,
A pledge to all mankind.
He has taken of earth's beauty
One strand of every hue,
Or orange and green and purple,
Of red and gold and blue,
And hung them in a glorious arc,
A prism of delight.
Beyond the reach of desecration,
God's covenant with man
is sore within him now.
Too long the storm has raged abroad.
The sky has been dark with clouds.
So now he rents the veil apart
And writes with streams of colored light
His message in the heaven:
He will no more destroy the earth.
A double promise, doubly given.

Margaret Mary Jones Strope

Two Prayers of Thanks

I

I thank you, Lord, for what I have;
My house, my car, my boat.
My G. M. stock is doing fine.
My wife likes her fur coat.
I saw such misery last week
On my trip around the earth.
I realized how fortunate
I am to have such worth.
I felt such joy in church today,
So good to be alive,
That when they passed the mission plate
I tossed the man a five.

I thank you, Lord, for things I've had;
My hut, my cart, my goat.
And when the river rose last week
I'm glad I stayed afloat.
At first I felt such misery,
When my husband left this earth,
But he is in a better place
Than he has been since birth.
I felt such joy in church today,
To be part of Your plan,
I took a five centavo coin
And gave all that I can.

Mahlon Brewster Strope, Jr.

There Is A God

"There is no God!"
I know not whence the darksome thought
had come. I know I fought
to thrust it in some chamber dark
whence ghostwise it came creeping back.
Till at last, grown weary from the strain
of doubt that filled my troubled brain,
I took it from its hiding place,
resolved to meet it face to face.
If it be true, admit the truth
or put the lying thought to rout.
Brave words to start my searching with.
But alas! They proved my God a myth.
Myopic vision could not see
the One who had created me.
So like "the fool" did I become
that I concluded there was none.
Of what use then for me to pray?
My reason forced my heart to say:
"There is no God."
"There is no God!" I said again.
Then stood appalled at what it meant.
No strength or comfort anywhere.
My world was dust and black despair,

as stripped of all I once had known
denying God I stood alone.
And saw that life had lost its plan,
unable to find the why of man.
Then spoke a voice from Heaven above,
"Know ye not that God is love?
Warm and alive in the heart of man?"
Deny that love exists who can?
Creation's beauty all alone
should give the lie to those who moan,
"There is no God."
I moved my lips to one on high
Whose being I had dared deny.
I raised my head, the world grown bright.
A child of God had seen the light
and never more will ever doubt.
"There is a God!"

Margaret Mary Jones Strope

Poet's Prayer

Give me the words
The beautiful words
The words that linger
In forgotten dreams

Give me the words
The flowing words
The singing, soaring,
Soul-searing words

Give me the words
The life-changing words
The laughing, crying,
Truth-telling words

Give me the words
The beautiful words
Before my mind
… goes dark

Ivan Floyd Strope

Compelled

While yet in mortal body bound
I shall the wonder of His love
Share with all who gather 'round
Drawn to the Lamb by the Dove

Ivan Floyd Strope

Bugs

Lord, I have lived this life like a firefly in the spring
Lighting my own little section of the darkness
Like a butterfly decorating the summer garden
Like a bug on a flower
Finding a lady bug or two or more
To spend the long summer nights with.
Now fall is here and winter almost upon me
Let me not die with a broken wing and crippled antenna
Crawling under some rotting leaf to die alone
Rather let me go out flying full tilt
Like a bug on a windshield.

Mahlon Brewster Strope Jr.

Lightened Load

I haven't the strength of my youth
and can no longer bear the burden
of grudges and regrets.

Ivan Floyd Strope

DUI

For a six pack
He traded his life
He is mourned by
Three kids and a wife.

Mahlon Brewster Strope Jr.

Hope

Without Hope the spirit dies
having given up the struggle
In a shallow grave it lies
awaiting the body's arrival

Unaware of Hope's demise
the hollow host may strive for years
an animated living lie
surrendering to all its fears

Hope whispers to be heard above
the daily din of death and strife
and breathes the message of His love
and sings the story of His life

Fear not the one whose steed is pale
The Advocate has shed His pall
Sheltered within His crimson veil
now enter bold the judgment hall

Clinging to His crucifixion
rejoicing in His resurrection
offering the sole protection
from the terror of rejection

Ivan Floyd Strope

Shadows

Shadows shudder at His approach
His light reveals the perfect plan
Condemning sin without reproach
Defeating Death, behold the Man

Ivan Floyd Strope

Knight of the Realm

Hark ye now to my tale of olde
of princesses and knights so bold,
herald's horn and battle's clamor,
dragon's breath and tarnished armor.

So many dragons I have slain.
Yet one leviathan remains.
He is my ancient enemy.
Also my oldest friend is he.

He skulks deep in my secret parts,
his hidden lair within my heart.
He sires many sons, you see
my heart's a dragon nursery.

Their roar and fire fills the air
to terrorize milady fair.
Assured eternal victory,
I battle each one dutifully.

A knight must never break his vow
and as I reflect upon it now,
dragon slaying will seem a small thing,
when I am called before the King.

Ivan Floyd Strope

The Years of Our Youth

The years of our youth
are as shouted poetry
clamoring to be heard
until we reach maturity
and understand
how much louder
is a whisper.

Ivan Floyd Strope

The Warrior

The Warrior rises in rage,
too quickly draws his blade,
yet knows not where to strike,
and so in grief he weeps
for the little ones.

Vengeance is his vow
but is not his to reap,
belonging to Another,
yet still he longs to fight
for the little ones.

His sword impatient waits,
seeking wrongs to right,
singing songs of blood,
searching in the night
for the little ones.

In his dreaded dreams,
he can hear their pleas.
Finally falling to his knees
he bows his head and pleads
for the little ones.

Ivan Floyd Strope

The Smallest Kindness

The smallest kindness that we do
Is like a votive candle lit
Before the Virgin, then forgot
The moment that the apse is quit.
And though the thought evaporates
Like holy water on the brow
The candle burning bright inside
Is like an unspoken holy vow.
And when our candle gutters out
And Darkness comes to claim its own.
We'll find our kindness candles light
A blazing stairway to his throne.

Mahlon Brewster Strope, Jr.

Departure and Arrival

Moved to tears
I gathered her in my arms
So frail
Tissue paper skin
White hair with scalp showing unprotected
A beautiful lady once
A beautiful lady now.

She was alone except for me
Where were her friends and family?
No one had come to see her out
I murmured tenderly
And kissed her face
And loved her as my own.

A little flutter and then a sigh
My tears dropped on her breast
But then I saw
She did not need them
But soared to great joy
And left me alone and in awe.

Joanne Lee Strope Pelton

Onward

We know not what the future holds
and barely half the past.
We can but trudge on day by day
until it's time at last.

Then trumpets blare and bright sun stream
and glory all around.
All warm and peace and joy shall be
and perfect love surround.

Joanne Lee Strope Pelton

The Run Home

He wasn't very good and seldom got to play.
But, still he longed for that perfect day.
It would be the bottom of the ninth with two men out
and up to him to win with clout.

But it never seemed to happen that way,
although he practiced faithfully
and slumbered with his glove of dreams.
There was just the dust and sweat that streamed
from his youthful brow beneath the cap
that proclaimed his allegiance to the team.

Then came a sultry summer day,
when Dad was there to watch him play.
An easy out flew true to him.
With a flair he snared and threw it in
and sneaked a peek into the stands
and there was Dad with clapping hands.

It wasn't the ninth but the top of the eighth
when his redemption floated across the plate,
a gift from the God of baseball and boys
and grown men who never gave up their toys.

He swung his bat with all his might
and to his wonder and delight
he heard the sweet sound of hardwood on horsehide
and he circled the diamond with pride.

But rounding third his vision blurred
with tears of joy
as above the host he heard Dad boast,
That's my boy.

Ivan Floyd Strope

Your Choice

Life itself can't bring you joy
Unless you really will it.
Life provides just time and space-
It's up to you to fill it.

Mahlon Brewster Strope, Jr.

Hidden Heroes

I almost missed him.
He was hidden in humility,
an unobtrusive old man,
handing out sale papers.

Standing off to the side,
just inside the entrance,
corralling wayward shopping carts,
supplementing his survival.

I noticed his hat,
the one with all the buttons
and concealed in the clutter,
the eagle, globe and anchor.

No doubt my mission
was most urgent,
wasting tomorrow's wages
on nothing of importance.

But somehow I was drawn
to the golden emblem,
for I too claim the right
to wear it as my own.

I met a hidden hero,
whose fading eyes had witnessed
the raising of Old Glory
over bloody Iwo Jima.

I wonder just how many
Humble, hidden heroes
cross my path each day
and silently fade away.

Semper Fidelis

Ivan Floyd Strope

Memories

A Tribute to Towanda High School Teacher, Miss Jean Holcombe

(Published in Towanda Daily Review in 1940s.)

"From Student to Teacher"
It was some few years ago
That I met you for the first.
I came to Senior English Class
Prepared to face the worst.
New faces all around me,
Not hostile it is true,
But still I felt so all alone
And then I looked to you.

That first gaze I must confess
Did not impress me much.
I did not see your inner self.
Just face and eyes and such.
But soon I found that there was more
Behind those rimless specs
Than just a pair of dark brown eyes
With humor in their depths.

I found in you a friend whose words
Of wisdom I still treasure
You taught, while teaching literature,
More else than I can measure.
Though long since I've left your classes
You still hold my high regard
For you've labored without ceasing
For no visible reward.

You have your time, your strength, yourself
To guide the adolescent.
We knew your heart was in your work
Though you were never effervescent.
You spoke with frank directness
Of honor, beauty, truth.
You sowed good seed on fertile soil—
The active mound of youth.

Year by year they pass before you,
Those clear-eyed youngster bright.
And year by year they must take with them
Knowledge greater far than might.
Do you perhaps grow weary sometimes
Of the constant strain
Their demands must make upon you?
Do you ever doubt the gain?

Then listen, Dear Miss Holcombe,
While I try to find a word
Which I feel will best describe you
By the praises I have heard.
It is not "sweet," nor is it "good,"
You are too brisk and far too wise.
Perhaps I'll just give up and say,
"You are an Angel in Disguise."

Margaret Mary Jones Strope

Mama's Gift

Mama was a teacher.
She taught us right from wrong.
She gave to us the guidelines
to help us all life long.

Mama's love was absolute,
All six of us the same.
With courage and with humor,
She faced life as it came.

Mama read to us at night,
Before we went to sleep,
The flash and flow of singing words,
A lovely gift to keep.

Joanne Lee Strope Pelton

Trophy

He threw a penny spinning
in the summer air
to twist slowly to the bottom
of Indian Creek.
Down we dove
in the goosebump depths
seeking glint of copper
on the rocky bed,
racing to be first
to rise dripping joy,
hand thrust high
clutching Daddy's praise.

Sandy Strope Hill

To a Sick Mother

Needle-thin nights
I lay awake
staring into futility,
making my childish bargains with God
while you coughed out your dreams
in the next room,
light-tears away.

Sandy Strope Hill

Graduation

At last
your bedroom is neat.
The vacuum has eaten your noise.
Sunlight plays gently on the waxed wooden floor.
No books to trip over,
tapes to kick aside.
No mound of jumbled jeans and T-shirts.
Lined up, stuffed unicorns and bears
stare at me solemnly.
The room speaks of silence.
Perhaps I will throw a pillow on the floor.

Sandy Strope Hill

The Parade

Memories spill out of his pen
and splash upon a field of white
memories from long ago
images still bold and bright.

He sees a child garbed with love
in old worn clothes, yet spotless clean,
on a second-story balcony
with wide eyes sparkling
at the wonder of it all.

People marching far below
vivid colors and clashing sounds
assault his lofty perch
as row
upon row
of people
march below.

And then there comes the huge round sign
red, white and blue with writing on
that his untrained mind cannot discern.
So to the source he turns
to ask a child's question.

"Mama, what does it say?"

*"Why child, it's almost Election Day
and that great man will win I'm sure
for he's a hero and knows the way
to make us all secure."*

She explains it to him carefully
although Daddy disagrees
Mama seems to like this Ike
and smiles as she tells her tyke.

But the child doesn't care.
Politics is not his fare.
He watches as they march away
and hopes they'll march another day.

Ivan Floyd Strope

Daughter

You can drive me wild
My little pixie child.
But when you're curled in sleep
My heart's too full to speak.

Sandy Strope Hill

Fossil Creek

Two hundred million years you kept your secrets,
washed by slow time to emerge into now.
Fossil shells from shores beyond time
waiting for our eager hands.

Sandy Strope Hill

On Raising a Daughter Late in Life

I watch her with a critical and jealous eye
My naive, nubile teen-ager
Flying gracefully to answer the phone
Knowing some hormone-ravaged teen-age jerk
Is calling to promote himself into her affections,
Knowing someday he or one of his ilk
Will succeed and take my baby away,
Forever away, from my care and protection.

What can she know of the pain
That comes with every joy,
Of the ecstasy of true love shared in wedlock
Of dirty diapers and snotty noses
Of kitchen drudgery and unpaid bills
Of hospital vigils at two a.m.
Of waiting up in trembling fear
For a drunken spouse to come home?

And so she also watches me.
She knows that I with my grayed hair,
My arthritic knee, weak heart and one deaf ear
With my edicts, decrees and restrictions
Can know or remember nothing of youth
Of the sheer joy of song, of dance, of living.
But I do know, I remember, and I care.

Mahlon Brewster Strope Jr.

I Remember

I remember the little house
Against the forest wall,
The dirt road where I spent my youth
When I was very small.

The honey bees in buckwheat fields,
A pheasant on the lawn,
The orchard where a white-tail deer
Would bring her little fawn.

The lightning crack of thunderstorms,
Our tin roof in the rain
And lightning bugs on humid nights,
A whip-poor-will's refrain.

Oatmeal for the morning meal
With homemade bread for toast
And maple syrup from the trees,
But I remember most,

My father playing catch with me,
The loving words he said,
My mother's kiss upon my cheek
As I lay down for bed.

Mahlon Brewster Strope Jr.

Teen

Like a teeter-totter
My teenage daughter.
Dreaming, teeming,
Sometimes steaming.
Growing, glowing.
(My love is showing.)
Life's a whirl
With my teenage girl.

Sandy Strope Hill

Gone But Not Forgotten

2:06 A.M.
Sleep eludes.
Conquered memories
resurrect.

Before alcoholics,
there were drunks,
no anonymity,
no steps.

50 years past,
or was it yesterday?
The big hand flashed out
striking the small boy's face.

Must have been something
the boy did or said
or maybe it was
just because.

2:07 A.M.
Sleep eludes.

Ivan Floyd Strope

Arguments of Others

I wake to a violent quarrel.
The rain had lashed itself to the back of the wind for a free ride.
I heard the wind shriek furiously and twist and turn.
The rain was thrown against my window and bones rattled.
Then silence.
Then back again in another bucking, raging gust.
I listened for a while and then grew sleepy.
My house was stout, my windows strong.
I snuggled down in my blankets,
Warm, dry—safe from their frightening lack of manners—
This time!

Joanne Lee Strope Pelton

Fairyland

It was a fine, warm, springtime day.
The sun was dropping low
And clouds all yellow, pink and red
Had set the sky aglow.

My grandchild asked, "Are fairies real?"
And, "Where do fairies stay?"
I took her to my flowerbeds.
"Here's where they hide away."

"They lurk among the hollyhocks.
They hide in foxglove blooms.
You'll see them, Princess, in the rose.
Rose scents are their perfumes"

With dancing eyes she stooped and looked
And played at peek-a-boo.
"I see a fairy there," she said.
Said I, "I see one too."

Mahlon Brewster Strope Jr.

The Place of Baseball

I remember Dad as
A man not often home
When I was young he soldiered
At Anzio and Rome

Then, in my grade-school years
And on through senior high
Dad was full of work and beer.
He seemed a passerby.

We lived in an old shack
With no utilities
And in the winters used
Outside facilities.

But still our home had love
With Mother always there
And evenings Dad relaxed
In his favorite chair.

Many, many years ago
Dad passed from this life's stage
I recall him now from
My vantage point of age.

But all my memories of Dad
Just one stays clear to me,
The only time in all my life
My Dad played catch with me.

Mahlon Brewster Strope Jr.

My Angel

The God who sees each sparrow fall,
Who lilies of the field has dressed,
Who in His wisdom made us all
Has called my baby to his rest.

Now he is in a better place
Then I, perhaps, shall ever be;
For now he sees God face to face
In innocence and purity.

Oh, pray for me, my little one,
That I may join you in that place
And gaze into the shining sun;
Stand by your side, and see God's face.

Mahlon Brewster Strope Jr.

When You Were Crazy

You look at the crib, a giant fib, and say
"Hello, Baby."
But there is no baby, only an empty bed.
I watch congealed, a frozen salad, while you talk to invisible infants
and I quiver, shiver in my mold.
I cry the baby inside me
while you talk (oh and oh, oh no, not so)
to nothing.
I like awake and shake and break.
I awake in my dream,
a silent scream
with you in your pain
again and again,
and I a child meek and mild, weak and wild,
with a scare in the air
to see you talk
to nothing.

Sandy Strope Hill

Family Reading Time

Your words flowed over us,
a river to carry us along,
Huck Finns on a raft of classics,
journeying through the mind.

Asthma, the doctors said,
coughs that shred the listener,
ragged cotton handkerchief pressed
close to gasping lips.
Finally, silence.

The raft journeys on.

Sandy Strope Hill

Flood in the Night (Age 13)

Rain had come to the little town
And heat had melted the snow.
The river rose to the danger point
Not many an hour ago.

The village slept 'neath a diamond sky
And all was calm and still
As a dragon crept toward the sleeping town
With infinite craft and skill.

Through the silent streets crept a yellow tongue
As a murmur changed to a roar.
The village stirred, but knew too late
That death was at the door.

Daylight came to the hamlet small
And with it the water's roll.
A blanket of yellow enfolded the town.
The serpent had taken its toll.

Sandy Strope Hill

Study Hall (Age 13)

Somewhere the kids are laughing.
Somewhere a child is gay,
But Study Hall at school
Is ruining our day.

Oh once we were so carefree
And happy as a clown.
But now we sit in silence;
The teacher has clamped down.

We must sit in quiet
While somewhere children play,
For Study Hall at school
Is ruining our day.

Sandy Strope Hill

Spring (Age 15)

Poets write that spring is grand.
I don't think that's so
Because I always seem to find
Mud wher'er I go.

In school I feel so sleepy,
Each passing hours a bore.
What I'd give if I could go
Home to sleep and snore.

"In spring a young man's fancy
Turns to thoughts of love."
I guess that writer never heard
Of a baseball bat and glove.

Yes, it's true that in the spring
Grass and flowers grow.
But as far as I'm concerned.
There's mud where'er I go.

Sandy Strope Hill

Remorse (Age 16)
(Written upon being denied permission to attend an event because of bad weather.)

The rain came down like pitchforks
And spoons and plates and knives.
The people who were in it
Were running for their lives.
Among these poor, poor people
Were Mother and dear Bean,
But they were hit by a pitchfork,
The largest ever seen.

As they died they murmured
In voice so sad and low,
"Forgive us please, dear Sandy.
We should have let you go."

Sandy Strope Hill

Helpless (Age 35)
(Written after Rick Baker's death)

If I could take your pain,
I would.
If I could ease your strain,
I would.

But where grief takes you,
I can never go.
What pain racks you,
I can never know.

I love you, love you, love you.
I can never tell how much.
And yet I stand struck helpless
By sorrow I can't touch.

Sandy Strope Hill

Humor

Untitled
(Published April 26, 1949, in Towanda Daily Review)

I am slowly going crazy;
Yes, I'm slowly going nuts.
I'll soon be cutting paper dolls
Without any ifs or buts.
My days have turned to nightmares
And my nights have turned to day.
I think I'm going cuckoo;
I just can't go on this way.
They will take me down to Danville
This next week or the next,
And put me in a padded cell
Where I will get some rest.
The reason I will tell you—
I'm not thinking 'bout the car.
Food coupons and rationing
Don't faze me any more.
My conscience doesn't bother me
And I haven't any ill.
I have no withholding tax to pay,
No income blank to fill.
I'm not worried about money
Nor investments I have lost.
no, the thing that drives me nutty—
Is four kids with whooping cough.

Margaret Mary Jones Strope

The Archer

(Written for Marvin Bernard Strope on the occasion of his 1st national
archery championship.)

He shot an arrow into the air.
It came to earth he knew just where.
Another arrow left the string.
Again his shaft pierced the x-ring.

For two whole days his arrows flew
into the bull's-eye straight and true
and when at last the meet was done
the championship again he'd won.

Mahlon Brewster Strope, Jr.
Which just goes to prove that old archers never die, they just
shoot the bull.

Limerick

We know that limericks are bawdy
and we don't like things that are tawdry.
But I like the timing
and I am just trying
to write one without being naughty.

Ivan Floyd Strope

Pet Peeve

I once had a cat
whose name was Attila.
But I called him At,
as it fit the fella.
The problem with At
was, "Where to put him?"
For he always sat
where it suited his whim.
I never could tell
where was that darned cat
and often I'd yell,
"At, where are you At?"

Ivan Floyd Strope

What Good Are You, Baby?
(Written for Mahlonna at her one-month birthday.)

Canst thou do anything? Canst Not!
Except to soil your pants a lot.

Canst catch a ball or shear a sheep?
Canst not; for mostly you just sleep.

When you're awake you're on the teat.
You sleep, you wake, you cry, you eat.

Canst thou do anything? Canst not.
Except to make us smile a lot!

Mahlon Brewster Strope, Jr.

Mosquito

Mosquito is an honest sort
She knows what she's about.
You have red blood inside of you
She wants to take some out.

One crimson drop is all she needs
And you don't feel a thing,
Until her spittle starts to itch
And burn and smart and sting.

One further fact that you should know
If you are really wise,
That only girl mosquitoes bite
The boys are harmless flies.

And occult also is this truth
The boy mosquitoes whine
While girl mosquitoes make no sound
So they can freely dine.

So if, when camping in your tent,
Mosquito wings you hear,
Ignore them and go off to sleep
But if there's silence ... fear.

Mahlon Brewster Strope Jr.

Heartbeat

My heart is a
percussion instrument,
thumping out a
solo symphony in
cadent jubilation
or sometimes
serenading in
soporific syncopation,
while I write poetry in
allegoric alliteration.

Ivan Floyd Strope

Little Line

A simple little line
Running through my mind
Recurring in my head
Forced me from my bed.

You cursed little line
I was sleeping fine.
You broke my writer's block
But, just look at the clock.

Oh wretched little rhyme
Don't you know the time?
My eyes are now all red.
I'm going back to bed

Ivan Floyd Strope

Bad Memory

I cannot recall.
Did I forget to remember
or remember to forget?
No matter. It's gone.
Which, as I recall,
was my intent.

Ivan Floyd Strope

Age 50

The mirror says it's so,
but my heart doesn't know.

Sandy Strope Hill

Where?

I couldn't find it.
Didn't know where it was.
The tattered old cover,
patched with black tape,
was nowhere in sight.
I needed to research
a secluded verse
and so I searched.
As always, it was hidden
where it was abandoned,
much to my chagrin,
covered with dust.
Where had it been?
Where had I been?
Was I back again?

Ivan Floyd Strope

Virtual Starship

On starship berthed in virtual bay,
the Captain enters his commands,
his orders instantly obeyed,
by silicon sailors' electronic hands.

Haul in the gangplank to reality.
Let loose the last lingering line.
Cast off all ties to banality
and for a while forget the time.

His ethereal vessel obeys her helm
and sheds her earthly mooring,
glides into his surreal realm,
all laws of physics ignoring.

Warp four, warp five, warp six he cries.
But then he hears a warning chime.
On to the bridge his mother strides,
"Shut off that thing; it's suppertime"

Ivan Floyd Strope

In Defense of Rhymes

Unrhymed is all the rage,
And I would not dismember it.
And yet—perhaps it's age—
I really can't remember it.

Sandy Strope Hill

The Engineer and the Poet

The Engineer commands correctness
both of rhythm and of rhyme.
The Poet seeks just beauty
resting softly on the mind.

Precision and perfection
want to rule the verse.
As the Muse plays coy and fickle
and refuses to converse.

As they wage their weary war,
the page is blank before me.
Who would think it is so hard
to compose a little poetry?

The Engineer and the Poet,
it seems will always be
locked in disagreement
and eternal enemies.

Which will win the battle,
I can hardly say.
I just want to write it
before the end of day.

Ivan Floyd Strope

Of Ants and Men

One day, while sitting on "the throne,"
Quietly and all alone,
Pondering long on things extant,
Both large and insignificant,

Surrounded by a room of stone,
And steel and glass and porcelone,
I saw beneath my very pant
A little, tiny, crawling ant.

At first my thoughts would not condone
This creature from some other zone.
I moved a foot intolerant,
And stepped with step most confidant.

The ant, not one to be undone,
Hid in a seam within the stone,
And so I tried another slant;
I doused it with expectorant.

The same results, I should have known.
So now I blew 'till it was blown
upon its back (it was flipp-ant),
Still it ignored its assailant.

It got back up with ant-like groan
And went on seeking crumb of scone,
And so at last I did recant;
Called off my war upon the ant.

One thing I had at last been shown
Is that, sometimes we moan and groan:
We carry on and rave and rant
o'er things too insignificant.

Mahlon Brewster Strope, Jr.

Breaking 100

It's strange the way that golfers count,
Their sums seem rather lax.
They're always on the green in three
While two putts are the max.

A ball struck out of bounds appears
by magic, back in play;
Yet, not one extra stroke is claimed,
A lucky bounce they say.

A ball that lands behind a tree
Is, happily, just clear;
From in the thicket out it flies
But no sound can you hear.

Now 'Mulligan' has played more golf
Than any pro on earth,
He always hits it terribly
Yet takes not one stroke's worth.

And so it goes for eighteen holes
From rough, to pond, to fence.
If golf is a relaxing sport,
Why are the players tense?

Well, I play golf the honest way
And though my drives go hooking,
I never cheat in any way,
Except when no one's looking.

Mahlon Brewster Strope, Jr.

My Unwarped Brain (Age 19)

Too much thinking warps the brain,
Or so the witty say.
Looks like there's no danger,
At least—not right away.

Sandy Strope Hill

Fishing Fun
(Written for a friend whose husband loved to fish.)

I bought a worm to catch a fish.
I thought it would be easy.
But I find I can't get hold of it;
The little critter's greasy.

It squirms and squiggles, twists and turns
And wraps around my fingers.
And even when I've thrown it down
The odor of it lingers.

I put my foot upon its tail
To hold it in the boat,
Then take the hook just by the eye
And drag it cross the throat.

Hooray! it works, it's on the hook.
I look at it and frown,
Then flip it in the water quick
And hope that it will drown.

Then just as I am settled back
And reaching for a drink
My rod tip jerks and doubles up.
I've got a fish, I think.

I grab the rod and spill my drink.
My heart begins to race.
I jerk real hard. A fish flies up
And hits me in the face.

And now I fear that I must try
To take it off the hook.
It flips its tail and stares at me,
A wide-eyed, fishy look.

With thumb and finger and great care
And thinking, "Oh, God, why me?"
I pick it up and then I find
That fish, like worms, are slimy.

It slips away out of the boat
But that suits me just fine.
Besides it is too small to keep
So I just cut the line.

My husband turns and looks at me
And reaches for a beer.
And as he turns his back again
He says, "Ain't this fun, dear?"

And I just let the hookless line
Down in the water lie,
And take my book and settle back
And watch the clouds sail by.

Mahlon Brewster Strope, Jr.

Fishing Fun II

They were aged ten and eight and four.
The youngest had not fished before,
Down to the family fishing pond
Where ducklings quack and swim around,

Where seagulls squawk with raucous cries
And wheel and soar in bright blue skies.
The older boys with fierce intent
Most eagerly to fishing went.

They cast their lines out side by side.
Each watched the other's cork and vied
To catch the first, the best, the most
And thus to gain the right to boast.

The little girl stood on the rocks
And freed her toes of shoes and socks.
Into the pond she plopped her feet
And on a flat stone took a seat.

Most awkwardly she cast her line
Purchased cheap at the five and dime.

Then turned to watch a butterfly
Go flitting through the summer sky.

She bent to watch the pollywogs
That someday would turn into frogs
And wondered how a slimy kiss
Could somehow make a frog a prince.

Now something jerked hard on her line.
Then she jerked back and just in time.
Of course, you know what came about;
Out flew a glist'ning twelve-inch trout.

Her brothers rushed about to see
With both surprise and jealousy.
She grasped the trout with two firm hands
While both the boys made their demands:

"Let's put it on the stringer quick."
"Let us hold it. Is it too slick?"
But the little one with lip a-pout.
Took the fish and turned about

She threw it back into the lake
And said, "Oops. That was a mistake."
"How could you throw the fish away?"
"Cause it will be a prince some day."

And last of all she got her wish.
She bragged, "I caught the biggest fish."

Mahlon Brewster Strope, Jr.

Untitled

Tickling the sage,
up the winding trail
The pickup goes bumpity bump,
I wish we had sails

Marvin Bernard Strope

Haiku

Haiku is a Japanese form of short poetry, containing three lines and seventeen syllables, with the first line having five syllables, the second line having seven syllables and the third line having five syllables. Haikus do not have to rhyme and seldom do. Haikus usually include a season word (kigo). Senryu is similar to Haiku in construction. During the 18th century this form of Haiku was developed by Karai Senryu (1718–1790). However, Senryu tend to be about human nature while Haiku are about the natural world and often love. Unlike Haiku, Senryu do not need to include a kigo. A poet who writes in this style is known as a Haijin.

Poetry

Poetry distilled ...
whatever is in the heart
spilling from the quill

Ivan Floyd Strope

Red Redemption

Night ... black as my sin
Yields grudgingly to Son rise
As red as His blood

Ivan Floyd Strope

Special (for Tyler)

He was born special.
Therefore, he is not able
to limit his love.

Ivan Floyd Strope

Realization

I once was content
'til I realized, I was
simply complacent.

Ivan Floyd Strope

Of Princes and Frogs

Don't expect a prince
When you are romancing frogs
What you kiss ... you get

Ivan Floyd Strope

Tools of the Trade

Insurmountable
By prayer and perspiration
Reduce to rubble

Ivan Floyd Strope

Epiphany

Oh, how could it be?
At last, I finally see.
It's not about me!

Ivan Floyd Strope

Healthy, Wealthy & Wise

Laughing at myself
Tonic for my ego's health
Imparts wisdom's wealth

Ivan Floyd Strope

Joy

Few folk realize
That love is a decision
And joy a surprise

Ivan Floyd Strope

Eternal Now

Time was not until
He spoke it to existence
From eternal now

Ivan Floyd Strope

Pigtails & Inkwells

I know what to do
to show her my love is true
I'll turn her hair blue

Ivan Floyd Strope

Warming Trend

A simple smile
The warmth of words from her heart
Bring spring in winter

Ivan Floyd Strope

Hidden

Past my stoic shield
Behind many barriers
Feelings are concealed

Ivan Floyd Strope

Three Haikus

A little flower
Blue with a yellow center
In a concrete crack

Bird feeder, squirrel
Flicking a gay bushy tail
Angry jay diving

Floating yellow leaf
Grasshopper out for a ride
Quick, hungry trout. Slurp.

Mahlon Brewster Strope, Jr.

Fantasy

This poem was inspired by a famous image, of the Eagle Nebula, taken by the Hubble telescope. The Eagle Nebula is so named because it resembles an eagle in flight. It is found in the constellation Serpens (The Serpent). This is a two-part constellation; Serpens Caput (Serpent's Head) and Serpens Cauda (Serpent's Tail). Between the two parts is the constellation Ophiuchus, also known as The Serpent Holder.

The pillars of gas, located near the Serpent's Tail, are known as Towering Pillars or Elephant Trunks. The Star Queen and Her Throne is a much older name for this area. The pillars are formed from dense interstellar gas and are a star nursery. New stars are formed in this region, which is about 7,000 light years from Earth.

Star Queen

Where warriors guard
the Star Queen's throne
the Eagle ever flies
clutching at the Serpent's tail
to steal Ophiuchus' prize.

Eternal battle rages on
from dust to dying breath
as star song lulls the nursery
and infants come to rest
upon the Star Queen's breast.

Ivan Floyd Strope

Star Dreamer

Her reach falls short and yet she reaches
to grasp that which she can not hold,
yearning for those stardust beaches
and seeking for those suns of gold.

She knows in truth it can't be done
and yet she won't give up her quest.
She runs her race that can't be won,
pursues her goal with zealot's zest.

Her gaze is fixed on darkened skies.
She dreams of that which cannot be.
Away to points of light she flies
to land on shores she'll never see.

Joyful to the stars she flees.
To her foolish dreams she cleaves.
Believing what she cannot see
and seeing all that she believes.

She basks in warmth from foreign suns
and breathes air spiced with scents of night,
caresses silver sands at dawn
and bathes in rivers flowing bright.

She wanders where the star winds waft
nestled in her mindship's cradle,
practicing her dreamer's craft,
living out a child's fable.

Now who can tell what may yet be
possible for you to see?
What dream? What goal? What victory?
Yet first you must a dreamer be.

Ivan Floyd Strope

Starsong

Wafting on the starwind
her starsong beckons me.
She hides herself within
her haunting melody.

Her siren song she sings
to lure fools like me,
distracts from earthly things
to sail across her sea.

Looking into the past,
my stellar time machine
finds my lover at last
and listens to her sing.

I must her favors win,
as she calls coyly from
a new meridian
and summons me to come.

But it can never be.
Her lair is much too far.
Had I eternity,
I could not reach her star.

I am content you see
to gaze into the night,
caress her distantly,
hoping that I might,

someday eventually,
behold my destiny.
While listening to the night,
as starsong beckons me.

Ivan Floyd Strope

The Starwind's Cargo

(Originally published in The International Who's Who in Poetry 2004)

I've cargo bound for starports,
dreams cradled in my hold,
homesteaders bound for hard times,
young lovers bright and bold.

I've vast distances to travel,
uncharted voids to cross,
frontiers to be discovered
and fortunes to be lost.

I've young men fearing failure
with nowhere left to run
and foolish men thrill seeking
who think that dying's fun.

I've wanderers and teachers,
a potpourri of humanity,
criminals and preachers,
blessings and profanity.

I've unrepentant sinners
with heavy burdens loaded
and those fleeing persecution
by fear and hatred goaded.

I've cargo bound for starports,
hammers, saws and rope.
I've tools to conquer new lands.
But I mostly carry hope.

Ivan Floyd Strope

Flight of the Starwind
(Originally published in <u>The Silent Journey</u> 2004)

Suspended in her ethereal realm on high
like a trinket on God's yuletide tree
moored solidly to sturdy nothing
sheltered safely in her home world's lee

With hope, dreams and other necessities
stowed in her spinning outer ring
Spokes reach out from her central hub
to spread her shimmering skirts between

Her Captain issues his commands
to silicon sailors with digital hands
and rockets' flames consume the night
softly sending her from shadow land

She fills her subtle sails with streaming starlight
gathers the gale within in her gossamer grasp
persuaded by the searing gentle fury
launches her beauty into emptiness

Fleeing from her native star
within the photon flood flowing bright
wafting through eternal raging silence
she stately strides across the endless night.

Ivan Floyd Strope

Traveling

Someday I would like to travel—between time, that is—
I'd go back to when the giant lizards shook the earth and the air trembled
With their screams.
I'd move along with Lucy on the African veldt and watch our race evolve—
Faster than we suppose.
I might go up to the land bridge between Siberia and Alaska and watch
Mastodon and man stream onto a new continent.
I'd stay to watch the Indians glide through endless forests
But then I'd skip the next three thousand years or so
And pick up the trail when we go streaking to strange suns and find a
Thousand whirling planets to explore
And their people to understand.

Joanne Lee Strope Pelton

Home Star

A soft blue diamond
shimmering in the dark
our new home world
circling faithfully about
our new home star
quietly resting
on Orion's shoulder.

So many long years
riding our shining
chariot to the stars
propelled by
the breath of God
bone weary of boredom
tired of nothingness
hiding hope safely away
so as not to be lost
only found again.

Thinking not of those
who perished
waiting for dreams
to awaken
waiting, waiting, waiting.
Surely no worse fate
than to die waiting.

No more waiting
there through the porthole
blindingly beautiful
home at last.
Home where we
have never been before.
How strange that we
should miss it so.

Hear the engines' joyous roar
feel our comfortable cage
quaking beneath our feet
closer, closer, closer.
Our dreams
have awakened.

Ivan Floyd Strope

Third Moon Rising

Far away and not so long ago
the third moon rose in amber skies
as lovers quarreled far below
and fire flashed from blue-green eyes.

Golden seas caressed silver shores.
Harsh desert winds swept rust red sands.
Summer was spent and winter roared.
He held her heart in trembling hands.

Red sand mated with winter wind,
thus giving life to soft pink snow.
Yet desert wind cannot rescind
uttered words nor the seeds they sow.

Defeated by her strongest fears,
as pink snow fell on flaxen hair,
swirling around her frozen tears,
lofting love above on cold air.

"Why? Why? Why?" she quietly cried.
Sheltered within his crimson cape,
"Never again." He softly lied,
as he gently nuzzled her nape.

Ivan Floyd Strope

Unnecessary Journey

Once I wished upon a star,
wondering where off Earth you are.
Took a ship and raced through space,
but I never found a trace.
Back to Earth I went once more,
found you at my own front door.

Sandy Strope Hill

Starwind's Shame

My ship! My ship! My beautiful Ship!
What have they done to her?
Where once she carried hope and dreams,
now she cradles terror.

Her holds are crammed with Hell.
Her crew is bent on killing.
She has become the Queen of War.
Her conversion obscene and unwilling.

Her lovely lines, beauty sublime,
now terribly truncated,
with projecting purveyors
of death, desecrated.

Is infinity not big enough?
Why send our sons to die?
This planet was another's home
until it caught our eye.

Ivan Floyd Strope

Star Gazers

Stars like diamonds in the sky,
Shining in the night,
And gazing up I wish that I
Could take a magic flight.

I'd visit every star that shined
Throughout the galaxy,
Where other beings I would find
Just gazing up like me.

Mahlon Brewster Strope, Jr.

Aliens

UFOs aren't real, the scientists say.
What a shame.

Sandy Strope Hill

Nature

The Listening Tree

I walked into the deep woods
where I found my favorite tree
standing with his brothers
waiting patiently.

I sat beneath his shelter,
leaned back against his bark
and waited for the city
noises to grow dark.

Wind whispered ancient secrets,
which I could not discern.
For I tried too hard to hear
what I simply should have learned.

To rest in forest splendor
watching furry thieves
scamper in the branches
among the laughing leaves.

To glimpse a timid doe
with beautiful brown eyes
grace me with a visit
just as daylight dies.

Wind whispered ancient secrets,
as I began to learn.
Enjoy the time you're given,
each moment in its turn.

Ivan Floyd Strope

Autumn Wind

Maples poised against the sky,
Flocks of wild geese winging high.
Confetti leaves beneath my tread.
Tang of smoke and flash of red.
Memory's winds blow back and forth.
The mountains call. I must go North.

Sandy Strope Hill

Return

It was a grey November day when I
First met the sea—
She was the grey Atlantic and she swept
The soul from me!
I stood upon the slanting shore
And breathed the sharp salt air.
Grey sky met grey ocean
And stretched forever there.

The seagulls wheeled for my delight
And screamed their ancient cry—
The sullen ocean answered
With roar and sigh.
The breakers rolled in foaming white
And hissed about my feet.
Cold sand sifted out beneath me
Where sea and I did meet.

I watched the waves rush in again
And slide back out once more
And in some dim primeval past
I'd known this scene before.
I'd stood upon some shell-strewn beach
Upon some other sand
And known this same fierce feeling
When I was barely Man.

I shook my head back to the sky,
So lowering and grey.
It was a younger, filtered light that
I had known that day.
The same song surged within me
As hummed back in the past.
I looked upon the ocean
And received my love at last.

Joanne Lee Strope Pelton

Again Autumn

Once I sprawled sun-dappled
Under the burning tree
While shards of blue
Pierced me through
And maple rain fell all around.

Today, a maple called my name,
And startled autumn stirred
And rustled in my soul
With the same slow wonder.

Sandy Strope Hill

Vacations of the Mind

Around me, computers hum
And voices drum
While through my heart, a river flows
Pine trees preen with sudden snows.
And in my mind, home's mountains rise
While sunrise dawns behind my eyes.

Sandy Strope Hill

Greenwood

I walk into the greenwood
a gray woman
and sink into fragile moss.
Through gray sponge eyes
I soak up green light
slanting down the long afternoon
I feel glad wind
breathing warm on city skin.
I leave greenwood
grown green.

Sandy Strope Hill

Bridal Veil Falls

Mountain shedding tears
cold crystal cascade
pledged to riven rocks
subtle submission
to the water's will

Dancing drops of life
playful water nymphs
flashing in the light
floating in the mist
rainbow's radiance

Feast for hungry eyes
soft soothing sound
refreshing thirsty spirit
flowing to the heart
fills with gentle joy

Ivan Floyd Strope

Driftwood

Splintered, shorn of bark and limbs,
tossed by the stormy sea
above the reach of wind and tide;
a battered tree trunk makes me a seat
to watch the endless waves.

Its space in the far away forest
Has long been filled by eager saplings
which know nothing of the endless sea.
The battered driftwood trunk
has become its own coffin.

It provides a convenient seat
Where we both rest quietly, mutely
while small crawling creatures
inflict little injuries
finishing the job the sea has begun.

Mahlon Brewster Strope Jr.

The Hummingbird

There's a hovercraft in my garden
burning and blurring the air.

There's an emerald in my garden
winking from flower to flower.

A flashing green gift of a jewel
delighting my heart for an hour.

Joanne Lee Strope Pelton

The Hills (Age 19)
(Printed in National College Anthology of Poetry, 1959)

The hills of home are rolling hills
That laze in the sun.
Greenly rich with bush and tree,
They lie across the land.

The hills of home are craggy hills,
Above the river's bed.
They rise—steep, rock-ribbed, blue-green—
With cotton floating overhead.

The hills of home are paint-splashed hills
When autumn's brushes pass.
They slope above, around the town—
In varied hues lie massed.

The hills of home are everywhere,
From front porch, window, door.
The hills grow all around the town,
And I—I could not love them more.

Sandy Strope Hill

Spring Joy (age 17?)

The trees shake out in ecstasy
Their newborn budding green,
Displaying to their sylvan world
Their fresh spring dresses' sheen.

Perfumed with odors of new life
My leaping heart they snare.
And sunlight, glancing through the trees,
Softly strokes my hair.

Sandy Strope Hill

On Returning Home—A Sonnet (age 19)

Today I am as one alive again
For I beheld my high and windy hills.
Within me beauty is become a pain
That seeks to ease its aching in their still,
But vibrant form. The Susquehanna flows,
A sunlit stream below their velvet slope,
And twisting in and out o'er all the land it goes
To bind me by its turning silver rope.
Through these, my soul, reviving, seeks
The God of nature and of home-returning men.
Through wood and rill, He to my spirit speaks,
And deep within a flame is lit again.
Now I am whole anew and I am free,
So very deep are these a part of me.

Sandy Strope Hill

Snow Prayer

I took a walk in the newborn snow
that had come as a gift in the night,
while I slept in my heated cocoon,
and old magic had fallen in white.

I walked slowly, alone with the snow
and a great calm came to me.
I lifted my eyes and my heart
and embraced deep serenity.

I stood 'neath an old pine tree.
The light was filtered and dim.
I touched bare hands to its side
and felt the slow heartbeat therein.

A reverence touched my soul
for trees and snow and sky.
I heard the old gods speak to me
in sifting snow and wind's soft cry.

Joanne Lee Strope Pelton

Celtic Dance

The eye of the moon is on me
so luminous and bright.
I dance beneath her lantern
all through the summer night.

She sees the solstice steps I weave,
the gathering of power.
She watched three thousand years ago
when magic was in flower.

The eye of the moon is on me.
I bathe in her brilliant rain.
She hears my song so wild and pure
and the Goddess hears the same.

Joanne Lee Strope Pelton

Remnants

We trekked the trail in order of age
the eldest in the lead and as in birth
followed moments thereafter
by the middle son and then by me,
by several years the youngest one.

Up the rocky narrow path
beneath the searing soothing sun
the lean clean air not quite filling our laboring lungs
up, up always up above the towering trees
into the land of eternal snow
where wind and ice and rocks rule forever.

Our compass and our map proved true.
The lake was there, crystal blue
like a hidden velvet diamond
softly reflecting the glory of heaven.

We pitched our tents beneath the glow
of the burning golden sky
to watch the reaching alpine peaks
steal the sun from its home
to hold it captive 'til the dawn.

Then came the wind rushing down
from its lofty mountain height
as stars peeked out bold and bright
to herald the coming of the night.

We sought the fire's friendship then
and huddled around its dancing flames
and shared our many memories
of family and friends and fading names.

Then silently we saw
veiled within the dying coals,
remnants of ghosts long past
and on each face with sooty strokes
the fire brushed a shadow mask.

Ivan Floyd Strope

A Winter Walk through the Orchard

With greatcoat and galoshes
Shuffling slowly on three legs
I see a bare branch on the old apple tree
In a little twig fork
A single lonely apple
Funny little prune face
Under a snowy cap
Passed by the pickers
disdained by the deer
Still, on one cheek, a trace of red
But hardly an apple anymore
I wonder, will it last 'til Spring?

Mahlon Brewster Strope, Jr.

March Winds

I love the challenge March winds fling.
They shake my soul with such delight
I stand atop the highest hill
And love March winds with all my might.

Joanne Lee Strope Pelton

Storm

The night was wet and wild with wind.
Bare branches whipped and whirled away.
Above the road, oaks roared their rage
And all pines did shout and sway.

Joanne Lee Strope Pelton

Night Riders

I love and hate the strong nights
That come when autumn is here.
The full moon pours the white light down.
The bones of leaves go rattling round.
The dark clouds fly across the sky.
The ghostly riders thunder by.

Joanne Lee Strope Pelton

Butterfly

Gliding softly on the air,
As light as fairy breath,
The butterfly flits here and there
And never thinks of death.

With danger all his days are fraught,
From birds and weather too.
He flutters on without a thought,
As though all skies were blue.

Perhaps a man could learn something
From every butterfly,
And go through life on mindless wing,
While worries flutterby.

For Fate controls our pain and strife,
And all our consternation
Won't change one breath of bitter life,
Or change our destination.

All stress and worry are for naught
And love is only pain;
A trap in which two hearts are caught,
Without a chance for gain.

So like the butterfly I'll be,
By wind and weather tossed,
Forgetting ever I knew thee
Until the winter frost.

Mahlon Brewster Strope, Jr.

Potpourri

On the Beach

Eighty-two years have passed
Like a cloud on a distant hill they flitted by, unnoticed.
I recline on a plastic chair
Which my grandson has plopped down on the beach,
Saying, "Get a little sun, Grandpa."

There! A bouncy bikini blonde just breezed by-
Thirty seconds ago—and I forgot to look.
My mind was on another beach
It seems like a thousand years ago and a million miles away.
And yet it seems like yesterday.

The bloody surf is crashing
And the air is thick with bullets like buzzing bees.
Seeking to still my pounding heart.
I shift my position to ease my hip.
A piece of shrapnel makes it difficult to sit in one position too long.

A young woman approaches and plops an infant on my lap
"Watch Edgar for a while, Grandpa,"
She says, adjusting the big beach umbrella.
Edgar! What kind of a name is that for a man-child to bear?
And then I remember that is my middle name.

She smiles, showing her dimples, her eyes sparkling.
She looks like my dear Margo, gone these many years.
Ah! we strolled this same beach in the moonlight
And pledged our hearts and made passionate love on the sand.
I remember we used to bring Junior here.

And watch the endless surf while he dozed in his basket.
He searched for broken seashell treasures here.
He caught his first fish with me in this same surf
And walked with his girlfriend and I suspect
Pledged their love on the moonlit sand.

They own the condo on the seaside cliff behind me.
Two teenagers approach, strutting;
Full of themselves and their barbell biceps.
They bump the umbrella and the sun suddenly blinds me
"Put that back, please," I say.
"Do it yourself, Old Man,"

They smell of suntan oil and beer and sweat.
They begin to taunt.
A bronzed lifeguard approaches
And they are conveniently distracted by a pair of passing bikinis
Which I again forgot to notice before they were already by.

Tomorrow I shall rise at dawn and run five miles on the beach
And look for treasure the tide has left
And maybe fish the surf a while as I once did.
But for now I think I'll take a little nap,
On the beach. "Mickey, come and get Edgar."

Mahlon Brewster Strope Jr.

Thoughts

I knew I had the horse power when I was old enough to know anything.

—

I frequently rely on first impressions.

—

There they were. I think I called them.

—

Look, Bernie—a black deer!

Lynne Strope Jonas

Complicated

After reading my poetry
I have decided I must be
a very complicated man.
But then perhaps that was His plan.

How could wit and stupidity,
flowing with such fluidity,
combine with pain and joy and then
leak out of the very same pen?

Am I the sum of all my deeds?
Do demons on my spirit feed,
while angels wait with bated breath,
to rescue me from foolish death?

Am I the product of my genes
upon a stage with scripted scenes
and do I struggle to be free
from predestined eternity?

I'm sure He has a perfect plan
in which He lets me have a hand.
It seems He is my biggest fan
and I am just a common man.

Ivan Floyd Strope

The Advocate

Comes now a lawyer to the court
And claims his client does comport
Herself in manner right and mild
And knows how best to raise her child
She claims the father's into drugs
And runs with prostitutes and thugs.

A second lawyer with a snort
Stands forth and makes a sharp retort.
"The mother's story is obscene
My client is both good and clean.
While she is always on a "trip."
And beats the baby with a whip."

And while the parents thus contort
Pathetic stories for the court,
And act as though the child were bread
From each to have their egos fed,
The child, unheeded, sheds a tear
And lives confused in lonely fear.

Comes now the Guardian to the court
And files the facts in her report
And thus the judge with opened eyes
Sorts out the truth from all the lies
He grants the child a hopeful prayer
To grow in peace with love and care.

Mahlon Brewster Strope Jr.

Dream Journeys (Written in 1986)

My mind has gone asailing
On seas of childhood past.
Here be dragons, there be treasure,
Going home at last.

My heart has gone aroaming
To times I used to know,
Sifting through the years and tears
To touch the long ago.

My mind has found its reasons
As dreamtides ebb and flow.
But my heart has touched a child
And will not let it go.

Sandy Strope Hill

Balloons

My Fair balloons were blue and red.
"You hold on tight," My mother said.
"And do not let them get away,
I'll buy no more balloons today."

But they kept tugging on the strings
Like some poor captive living things;
So finally I set them free.
They rose up past the tallest tree.

I watched until they sailed from sight,
Then asked my mother of their plight.
"They'll burst and fall down from the sky
Like people when they aim too high."

"You won't be hurt if you stay low
And, when you fall, not far to go."
Well, what my mom said may be true,
But I'm not sure that is my view.

It's a better thing, perhaps to sail
Upon the breeze, although you fail.
I think my balloons will fly to Mars
Or even to the shining stars.

Mahlon Brewster Strope, Jr.

Struggling

I try to be philosophical in frustration,
Calm amidst chaos,
Brave in the face of the unknown
But
Sometimes I am illogical,
Wild
And
Afraid

Joanne Lee Strope Pelton

My Old, Flat Broad-Brimmed Hat

I've used my old, flat, broad-brimmed hat
For almost everything.
To keep the rain out of my eyes
And swat at things that sting.
To shoo a black bear from the path
There was nowhere to run.
I've flung it to the mountain breeze
To watch it sail, for fun.
I've filled the hat with blackberries;
The stains are on it still.
I've carried water for my horse
'til he had drunk his fill.
I've used my hat to shield a match
And get a fire lit
Before the bitter, wet north wind
Could snuff the life from it.
I don't go hiking much these days
But fish a placid stream.
I shade my face with my old hat
And fall asleep and dream.
But the very best of all the things
I've done with my old hat
Was catch my child a butterfly
To hold and wonder at.

Mahlon Brewster Strope, Jr.

My Old Hiking Boots

My old, cracked, worn-out hiking boots
have climbed a lot of hills,
across steep, bouldered, mountain slopes,
by quiet forest rills.

They've stopped beside a juniper
to watch the waxwings feed
and when a black bear came along
they really picked up speed.

I've waded icy snow-fed streams
and fished for alpine trout;
so many, many, long, long trails
with beauty all about.

The mountain trails still call to me.
they whisper in the breeze
but hiking's just a memory
with these arthritic knees.

Yet, just the other day, those boots
gave me one final treat
when they came stomping down the hall
upon my grandson's feet.

Mahlon Brewster Strope Jr.

On Dying

Let me die not of ale and age
Rocking with palsied hands in a darkened room;
And old dozing dog running rabbits by the fire.
Let me die on a high mountain,
Slipping, sliding into a glacial crevasse.
Let me drown in a raging rapids.
Let my heart stop while running a race.
Let me leave this world,
Naked as I came
In the arms of a lusty woman.

Mahlon Brewster Strope, Jr.

Wild Pitches

Words can be like baseballs,
Thrown hard and fast.
Some pitchers can throw
Over ninety miles an hour.

A ball can be lethal
If it hits the right spot,
Like your head
Or your heart.

Joanne Lee Strope Pelton

Consider Compromise

What would a man compromise,
if not his principles?

The art of compromise is a black art
practiced by the persuasive,
perfected by politicians and witches.

The spirit of compromise is an evil spirit,
making subtle introductions
to the spirit of defeat.

Compromise is oft disguised,
shrouded in the mists of neutrality.
If neutral be balanced,
it is a precarious position.

For neutral is gray,
without distinction,
without discretion,
without direction.

And it is in the gray
that men
lose their way.

Ivan Floyd Strope

Death of a Poet

So perfectly poetic,
that he should be
mourned in the rain.
The tears of the sky
gently cleansing
the stain of our pain.

We with shields held high
to fend off heaven
could not dissuade the drops
pledged to the ground,
lamenting their loss
with soft weeping sound.

As we lay our love
in flowered form
upon his tranquil breast,
one who loved him
slipped softly forth
to whisper his bequest.

With rhyme and rhythm
we chanted with her
the mantra of his love.
As heaven cried
the day he died
and tears flowed from above.

Salt-laden joy .
flowed from our eyes
to mingle with the rain,
as his words written
on our hearts
raised him up again.

Ivan Floyd Strope

Forever Seventeen

They have such fresh faces
One pretty and two handsome
Three faces reflecting
The invincibility of youth

The girl hoping
That someone
Will find her
Worthy of love

The boys trying
To be men
Like all young men
Fearing failure

Such wonderful faces
Proving there is still
Hope for tomorrow
With faces such as these

Three faces
Sharing a ride
Laughing and playing
And all talking at once

Three beautiful faces
Sharing the obituaries
How grotesquely out of place
Are their yearbook smiles

I knew them not
And yet I weep
For now they are
Forever seventeen

Ivan Floyd Strope

Gandy Dancer

Clink … Clink … Clink … Clink
steel … on … steel … on … steel
Clink … Clink … Clink … Clink
hammer swinging song
Clink … Clink … Clink … Clink
steel on wooden tie
Tamp … Tamp … Tamp … Tamp
stones to hold it on
Jack … Jack … Jack … Jack
rails are lifted high
Drip … Drip … Drip … Drip
sweat is streaming down
Drip … Drip … Drip … Drip
blistered back is bare
Clink … Clink … Clink … Clink
muscles ripple strong
Clink … Jack … Tamp … Drip
the whole hot day long

Ivan Floyd Strope

The Hands of Time

The hands of time sweep swiftly by
and in their many fingers fast,
the years and days and hours fly
and memories from moments past.

The hands of time are healing hands
and in their fleeting gentle grasp,
anguish and sorrow's subtle strands
can be severed and left at last.

The hands of time often hold strong
to regrets, remorse and sad songs
of how somebody did us wrong
and grudges carried far too long.

But did you know time is a sea
and slowly as the hours chime
burdens and pain can gently be
washed away by the hands of time?

Ivan Floyd Strope

The Dancer

He has passed beyond the veil
yet still their music lingers.
She hears his voice blend with the tones
of a solitary singer.

She holds his essence in her arms
and glides about the room.
The grace of sorrow rests on her
as softly as perfume.

Glistening eyes behold him still
as her fingertips caress
his handsome face with tender touch
and tears befall her dress.

Her friends hasten to console her.
Their efforts are in vain.
She whirls about with memories
dancing away the pain.

They watch her as she waltzes on
alone upon the floor.
Then silently they slip away
disturbing her no more.

Ivan Floyd Strope

Twilight Wolves

Circling 'round the waning light
Of those bent low with weight of years,
Cowards skulking in the night
Feeding off the mounting fears,

Of the frail, no longer strong,
Who should command respect,
Lingering in life too long,
Discarded victims of neglect.

Ivan Floyd Strope

The Duet

They carried the old man
to the edge of the autumn field
where they propped him up
in a too straight chair.

The old woman gave him a warm cup
and shaky hands raised it
to withered lips
as he sipped … just a bit.

Peggy and Tracker nosed about
looking for some fun
while the old man waited,
rested and listened.

Little long ears jumped up
and the jubilant hunters
began to sing their song,
the old man's favorite.

Peggy yipped joyfully
as Tracker, a true baritone,
bellowed from the basement
and the old man smiled.

The wrinkled eyelids closed.
The cup fell to the ground.
The hounds sang their duet
and the sun was warm …

… one last time.

Ivan Floyd Strope

Tick Tock

I had eternity
to indulge every whim.
My boundless energy,
I cast before the wind.

My fire blazed so bright,
no cares to rein me in,
concerned not for the fight
that I could never win.

Before the hands of time
stealthily stole away
my strength and youth sublime,
for they're the piper's pay.

So now my hair is grey.
Wrinkles beset my skin.
My strength has waned away.
My vision ever dim.

Although you may not hear
what I will say this day.
Turn down your music, dear.
I'll say it anyway.

Don't spend your strength on folly.
Don't waste your charm on sin.
Time is your enemy.
Old age awaits within.

Ivan Floyd Strope

Troll

From the silent shadows strode
a dreaded dark drenched troll,
by the name of Bitterheart,
and great blame did he impart.

The secret son of Thanknot,
raised in kindness he forgot,
midnight mayhem did he seek
and of anger did he reek.

Armed with spoken spears,
with which to heighten fears,
his victims he did spy,
to engage them with a lie.

Upon a slippery slope,
he sought to steal their hope.
Yet they with humble strength,
prevailed over him at length.

Finally overcome was he.
Frantic did he frightened flee,
as his onslaught was riven.
For him they had … forgiven.

Ivan Floyd Strope

The Game

The blood of my comrades
spills on the screen,
until the next frame,
when they jump up again.
Their death is only a game.
Play Station or play war
it's all the same.
They'll just jump up again.
Somehow, I remember it differently.
Oh well.
We must teach the young
how it was so much fun
in Hell.

Ivan Floyd Strope

Perfect

His furrows are straight
and perfectly parallel.
He never wavers,
never looks back.
He is on a mission.
Perhaps he misunderstood.

No, it's quite clear.
The admonition is
to be perfect.
An absolute,
if ever there was one.
Perhaps he misunderstood.

He labors under the burning sun,
but welcomes not its warmth.
The wind whips his body,
but he does not receive
the blessing of the breeze.
Perhaps he misunderstood.

His sharpened plow
tortures the fertile ground.
He plants his dead seeds,
which take shallow root,
yielding confused crops.
Perhaps he misunderstood.

Leaving love in his dirty wake,
he valiantly struggles on,
in his righteousness,
making perfect scars,
missing maturity.
Perhaps he misunderstood.

Ivan Floyd Strope

The Poet

His soul spills forth out of my pen
and splashes on a field of white,
simple words for seeking men,
words that he's compelled to write.

Compulsion seems to become him.
Poetry flashes in his eyes.
Beautiful words flow from within,
hues of truth not tinted with lies.

What possesses him to scribble
the meanderings of his mind?
Sometimes forcing thoughts to dribble.
Sometimes his quill leaves him behind.

In the wee hours of the morn
obsession keeps him from his bed.
Willful words from his heart are torn,
to be freed where his quill has bled.

Yet with tender trepidation
he writes unswerving to his goal,
with insightful inspiration,
reveal he must, his poet's soul.

Ivan Floyd Strope

Hide and Seek

Behind the trees of memory
waits a child, drawn back
in the lengthening shadow of years.
Waiting for someone to find him,
to laughing carry him home,
sit him down in a caneback chair,
feed him ice cream
tousle his hair,
and plant a kiss at the nape
of his bent, sweaty neck.
And yet he hides,
but rarely do we seek.

Sandy Strope Hill

Tribute

Old warriors in rigid formation
Raise their noise makers
To the empty sky
And honor the fallen

Smokeless powder leaves no trace
And the evidence of the salute
Soon fades away like thunder
Or some briefly passing life

Their white gloved hands
Gently grasp the widow's
And moistened eyes
Attempt to share the sorrow

Soon the field is empty
And a machine does
That which should be done
By comrades and friends

Not hydraulic fluid
But sweat should flow
Dirt piled one shovel at a time
Not back hoed in an instance

It is far too efficient
To have the void filled
By an uncaring machine
That never cries

He was made of
Blood and bone and feelings
Blood and bone and feelings
Should say, "Goodbye"

Ivan Floyd Strope

The Shadow of the Wind

Oh, how he tried to embrace the wind
But the tempest staggered
And reeked of gin

It growled and roamed and roared
And even when becalmed
It in a stupor snored

Yet still he yearned for loving tones
Deep within his heart
And buried in his bones

And she so frail and thin
Vainly sought to shelter him
From the shadow of the wind

Yet the wind is only air
Wafting where it will
There's really nothing there

Blowing wide and far
A never present ghost
How could it leave a scar?

The wind is spent and gone
Yet somehow it still casts
Its shadow dark and long.

Still love does not rescind.
If only he could yet,
Embrace the wind.

Ivan Floyd Strope

The Shared Feast

I cooked a meal of pain last night
and heaped my plate up high.
I brewed a pot of love gone wrong
and drank five cupfuls dry.

I left the dining table,
fierce burning pain within
and wandered weeping, room to room
until the night wore thin.

I bumped into a stranger,
whose anguished gaze met mine.
Then slowly I remembered,
I'd left some feast behind.

Joanne Lee Strope Pelton

Miss Lillian

Miss Lillian has gone to glory,
After years of helpless waiting.
Stiff of limb and mute of mouth, she pleaded
With her fierce dark eyes to let her go.
At first, we said no and put our hollow tubes
Into her pockets and kept her firmly with us.
But then we saw she was not truly living
And wished we had the power to let her go.
Grim year after grim year, we waited with her, mutual prisoners.
Finally, finally, he turned his eye to her and blinked
And so she soared to Him.

What took him so damn long?

Joanne Lee Strope Pelton

The Widowmaker's Song

(Originally published in <u>The Best Poems and Poets of 2004</u>)

Machine guns paint with tracer's glow
and sing the Widowmaker's song,
as mortars seem to fall so slow,
their lofty arc of death too long.

Then a comrade falls to the right
and to the left another's gone,
as muzzle flashes pierce the night
and sing the Widowmaker's song.

Reinforced by indecision
brave men cower in the kill zone,
as with militant precision
Death seeks and finds them each alone.

A man child in warrior's guise
surrenders life but Death declines
and as the warrior child cries
Death finds his friend, on whom he dines.

Then guilt claims the man child's soul.
Why my comrade and why not me?
As Widowmaker takes her toll
and demons dance and shout with glee.

As lifeblood feeds the thirsty ground,
a change becomes the warrior child.
Though hidden enemies surround,
He charges forth with rage run wild.

Is this then how heroes are born?
A man by grief and wrath beguiled?
No, if truth be known in the morn,
a hero's just a frightened child,

Ivan Floyd Strope

Merry-Go-Round

How subtly we're seduced
by the everyday mundane.
How easily beguiled
by the profound and profane.

Such slender graceful hands
sweeping round his face
veil the scheme of time
until it is too late.

Those little snips of life
ever lost to us each night
reflect the deeds undone
while waiting for the light.

As a greedy politician
wasting what was given,
we reach the end of things
and wonder why we're riven.

And when it's time to exit,
while standing at the door,
we ask, along with Ollie Twist,
"May I have some more?"

This carousel we ride on
offers a single chance.
So grab the brass ring first time.
There'll be no second dance.

Ivan Floyd Strope

The Box II

Inside me a box.
In the box, sorrow.
I think that I shall open
The lid tomorrow.

Sandy Strope Hill

Scent of Home

Tires crunch gray gravel
Old springs and squeaky brakes protest
The engine coughs to a stop
Wrinkled fingers find the handle

Twisting with a firm grasp
Un-oiled hinges announce his arrival
Shuffling around to open the trunk
He finds his cracked leather luggage

Not needing his direction
His feet follow the familiar path
Worn wooden steps
Embrace his slight weight

He reaches out to find
The friendly ancient knob
Beckoning from the door
That is never locked

He steps into the kitchen
And smiles when greeted with
Her gentle touch and
The scent of home

Ivan Floyd Strope

The End

At my funeral, when I die,
Will many come to mourn and cry?
Or will they curse and say, "At last.
Good riddance that his life is past."
But worst of all I think would be
If none came to remember me.

Mahlon Brewster Strope Jr.

On Turning Forty

There is in me a great clock ticking.
It's ticked for forty years.
I never heard these tones before.
I never felt these fears.

The clock is ticking faster now;
It's tripping double time.
It's speeding toward that final hour,
That one great final chime.

There is in me a great clock ticking.
I cannot slow its pace.
I know its rhyme and reason,
But when did it start to race?!

Joanne Lee Strope Pelton

Contentment

The fire snaps softly on the grate.
I stare mesmerized into the glow.

Outside sleet rattles against the pane
But my heavy drapes are snugly drawn.

The lamp shines on gently gleaming mahogany
My grey cat is curled on the couch.

The slow ticking of the mantel clock
Speaks quietly to me of peace.

I close my eyes and drift in absolute contentment.

Joanne Lee Strope Pelton

Long Anger

Anger can burst into sudden, startling
Flame, cool to cinders and all's over and done.

Or there's another kind—nursed slowly—
A banked bed of coals—fed and glowing
Quietly beneath the graying ash.

I'd rather chance the sudden singe
Than risk that long and steady burn.
Coal or flame,
The heat is not the same.

Joanne Lee Strope Pelton

Old Anger

If I let you out, will you shout?
Will you break your chain
Rampaging through my pain,
While I shiver, shatter
Like a crystal platter?

If I let you out, will you turn about
Whirl so sleek and fierce
To leap and pounce and pierce,
While I watch still caged
As you prowl enraged?

If I let you out, will you turn about?
Answer to command,
Caged on my demand?
Maybe you should keep.
Maybe you should sleep—for now.

Sandy Strope Hill

A Working Relationship

Housework and I are best of foes.
She stares as long as I can, hard,
She's even present from the line
I daily worship in the yard.

Housework and I are mistress and lover,
No need of binding vows have we.
The clothes to wash and fold and iron
Tell me I never can be free.

Housework and I are each back-patters,
I cook the meals, they taste so good.
I make the beds and smooth the spreads
And polish gleaming, deep-grained wood.

Housework and I are easy forgivers.
There is no do or die with us.
I run and laugh and hug my child.
She smiles rich through all her dust.

Housework and I are lax companions.
Sometimes we wave and pass each by.
The call of sun-sweet air is stronger
Than any call of dish to dry.

Joanne Lee Strope Pelton

Age 40

Thrown into the future,
the day I will die sails
on a slow boomerang curve
on its way back to me
by now.

Sandy Strope Hill

King's Pawn to King Eight

Dark as flowing blood,
dusk descending,
as a crimson flood,
o'er the field of ending.

Hurry, hurry dawn
bring to life the light.
Protect frightened Pawn
from never-ending night.

Clever, clever King,
silent subterfuge,
enchanting, luring
Pawn to be his stooge.

Diplomats, politicians,
and other practiced liars,
call for Pawns and guns
to fan the frenzied fires.

Pretty beauty Queen
to her Castle keeps,
posing for the King
as the kingdom weeps

Skilled in art of compromise,
sacrificing principles,
diagonally disguised,
Bishops spin their spells.

Clever, clever King
expects to win the fight,
prepares the Pawn to Queen.
But Pawn becomes a Knight.

Patient, patient Pawn,
beauty and finesse,
moving warriors on
both sides of the quest.

Checkmate

Ivan Floyd Strope

Index

978-0-595-47238-3
0-595-47238-9

www.ingramcontent.com/pod-product-compliance
Lightning Source LLC
Chambersburg PA
CBHW021144070326
40689CB00043B/1131